SEASONS OF FUN: SUMMER

SUMMER FUN

by Finley Fraser

Consultant: Beth Gambro
Reading Specialist, Yorkville, Illinois

Minneapolis, Minnesota

Teaching Tips

Before Reading

- Look at the cover of the book. Discuss the picture and the title.
- Ask readers to brainstorm a list of what they already know about summer. What can they expect to see in the book?
- Go on a picture walk, looking through the pictures to discuss vocabulary and make predictions about the text.

During Reading

- Read for purpose. Encourage readers to think about things that are special about summer as they are reading.
- Ask readers to look for the details of the book. What is happening?
- If readers encounter an unknown word, ask them to look at the sounds in the word. Then, ask them to look at the rest of the page. Are there any clues to help them understand?

After Reading

- Encourage readers to pick a buddy and reread the book together.
- Ask readers to name three things from the book that they can do during summer. Go back and find the pages that tell about these things.
- Ask readers to write or draw something they learned about summer.

Credits:
Cover and title page, © Rob Hainer/Shutterstock; 3, © Africa Studio/Shutterstock; 5, © FatCamera/iStock; 6L, © Pixfiction/Shutterstock; 6R, © Konstantin Faraktinov/Shutterstock; 7, © kali9/iStock; 8–9, © Air Images/Shutterstock; 10, © Siarhei SHUNTSIKAU/iStock; 11, © monkeybusinessimages/iStock; 13, © skynesher/iStock; 15, © Userba011d64_201/iStock; 16, © fstop123/iStock; 17, © Anton Starikov/Shutterstock; 18, © bhofack2/iStock; 19, © SerrNovik/iStock; 21, © Evgeniy Kalinovskiy/Shutterstock; 22 background, © S_Photo/Shutterstock; 22T, © Sergey Novikov/Shutterstock; 22M, © cjp/iStock; 22B, © PhotonCatcher/Shutterstock; 23TL, © Soloviova Liudmyla/Shutterstock; 23TM, © loveguli/iStock; 23TR, © monkeybusinessimages/iStock; 23BL, © sculpies/iStock; 23BM, © ze_pedro/iStock; and 23BR, © DaniloAndjus/iStock.

Library of Congress Cataloging-in-Publication Data

Names: Fraser, Finley, 1972- author.
Title: Summer fun / by Finley Fraser ; Consultant: Beth Gambro, Reading Specialist, Yorkville, Illinois.
Description: Bearcub books. | Minneapolis, Minnesota Bearport Publishing,
[2023] | Series: Seasons of fun: summer | Includes bibliographical
references and index.
Identifiers: LCCN 2022025650 (print) | LCCN 2022025651 (ebook) | ISBN
9798885093286 (library binding) | ISBN 9798885094504 (paperback) | ISBN
9798885095655 (ebook)
Subjects: LCSH: Outdoor recreation for children--Juvenile literature. |
Summer--Juvenile literature. | Play--Juvenile literature.
Classification: LCC GV191.62 .F73 2023 (print) | LCC GV191.62 (ebook) |
DDC 796.083--dc23
LC record available at https://lccn.loc.gov/2022025650
LC ebook record available at https://lccn.loc.gov/2022025651

Copyright © 2023 Bearport Publishing Company. All rights reserved. No part of this publication may be reproduced in whole or in part, stored in any retrieval system, or transmitted in any form or by any means, electronic, mechanical, photocopying, recording, or otherwise, without written permission from the publisher.

For more information, write to Bearport Publishing, 5357 Penn Avenue South, Minneapolis, MN 55419.

Contents

Hello, Summer! 4

The Story of Sandcastles 22

Glossary 23

Index 24

Read More 24

Learn More Online 24

About the Author 24

Hello, Summer!

It is time for summer fun.

The sun is shining.

It is hot outside.

Let's go find some fun things to do!

Some summer days, we go to the pool.

First, we need to put on our swimsuits.

Remember the **sunscreen**!

I wear a hat, too.

My brother likes to go to the beach.

We splash in the water.

Then, we build a tall **sandcastle**.

Sometimes, the water pushes it over.

Whoosh!

Say sandcastle like SAND-kas-uhl

Picnics in the park are fun, too.

We eat yummy sandwiches.

My mom brings ice cream.

Chocolate is my favorite!

My sister wants to fly a kite.

It has many colors.

We run through the grass.

The kite goes so high!

Let's play hide-and-seek.

My friend is the winner!

She always finds the best hiding spots.

My family goes **camping** in the summer.

We put a tent in the yard.

I bring out my sleeping bag.

Before we go to sleep, we have a **campfire**.

We toast marshmallows to make s'mores.

Yum!

A s'more

There are so many things to do during summer.

What is your favorite way to have summer fun?

The Story of Sandcastles

Some people believe the Egyptians made the first sandcastles. They made small **pyramids** from sand thousands of years ago.

In the 1850s, families in the United Kingdom started visiting beaches. They would build sandcastles.

Today, people make sandcastle art. There are even prizes for the best sandcastle builders!

Glossary

campfire an outdoor fire used for cooking or warmth

camping living and sleeping outdoors for a short time

picnics meals eaten outdoors

pyramids buildings with triangle-shaped sides that meet at a point at the top

sandcastle a small model of a building made from wet sand

sunscreen a cream that goes on skin to keep you safe from the sun

Index

beach 8, 22
campfire 18
camping 17
hide-and-seek 14
ice cream 10
sandcastle 8–9, 22
sunscreen 6

Read More

Fraser, Finley. *Summer Weather (Seasons of Fun: Summer).* Minneapolis: Bearport Publishing, 2023.

Murray, Julie. *Summer Adventures (Seasons: Summer Shine!).* Minneapolis: ABDO Kids, 2022.

Learn More Online

1. Go to **www.factsurfer.com** or scan the QR code below.
2. Enter **"Summer Fun"** into the search box.
3. Click on the cover of this book to see a list of websites.

About the Author

Finley Fraser is a writer living in Portland, Maine. His favorite summer foods are mint chocolate chip ice cream and very, very toasty marshmallows.